IN THE RED MEADOW

poems by carolyn stoloff

drawings by mildred thompson

new rivers press 1973

copyright © 1973 by carolyn stoloff and mildred thompson
library of congress catalog card number: 73-89342
isbn 0-912284-50-1

the author wishes to thank the editors of magazines in which the following
poems first appeared, for permission to reprint:
INVISIBLE CITY: "drawers open and winter escapes"
                  "Garbo's knees are gates. . ."
                  "evening, wedged in the door. . ."
                  "over a forest of coffins. . ."
THE NATION: "settling on tongues, owls close. . ?"
quotations from Arp reprinted here from ON MY WAY, POETRY AND
ESSAYS, by Jean (Hans) Arp, 1948, by permission of George Wittenborn,
Inc. New York, N.Y. 10021.

PREVIOUS BOOKS BY CAROLYN STOLOFF:

STEPPING OUT (unicorn press)
DYING TO SURVIVE (doubleday)

new rivers books are distributed in england by:
                philip spender
                69 randolph avenue
                london, w9, england
in the united states and elsewhere by:
                serendipity books
                1790 shattuck avenue
                berkeley, california
                94709

this book was manufactured at the print center, inc., 194 state street,
brooklyn, new york 11201 for new rivers press, p.o. box 578, cathedral
station, new york, n.y. 10025 in a first edition of 600 copies.

*"The world of memory and dream is the real world.
It is related to art, which is fashioned at the
edge of earthly unreality."*
          Arp — The World of Memory and Dream

*"enter the continents without knocking but with
a muzzle of filigree"*
          *Arp — Introduction to Max Ernst's
          Natural History*

Poems for MILLI

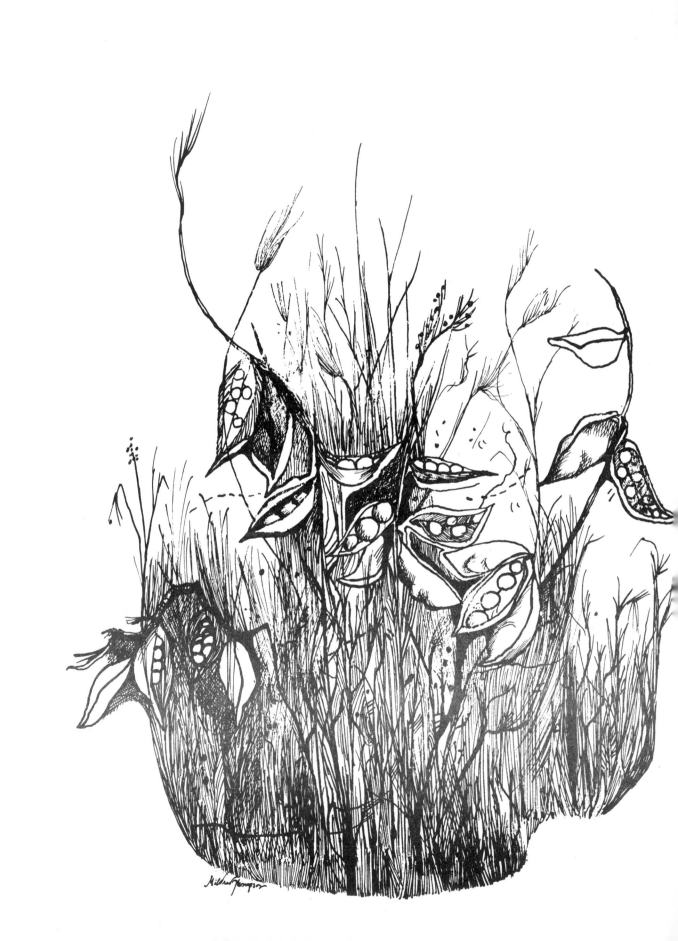

1.
wounds sing in the red meadow
   the morning gate swings idly on its hinge
      brides wake among wailing tongues
         pods open   white hair licks the wind

2.
stems bleed in the meadow
   light combs the milkweeds' silken hair
      reproach is a gate left open
         milky tongues idle on the wind

3.
brides rise in the meadow
   wings slip between the weeds shaking them
      morning opens its jaw reproachfully
         light licks the wailing stems

4.
wounds close   and pods and wings
   brides comb the wind with combs of grain singing
      the tongue will enter the gate again
         the red gate to the meadow

1.

drawers open and winter escapes
   statues cough
      wind wraps nurses in paper
         from whispering cornices infant faces
            fall among flowers of snow

2.

when nurses rub pedestals avenues open
   they enter
      winter is papered with faces   lost faces
         platinum hands break through
            clarinets blow   paper flowers escape in the night

3.

infants are rubbed   dreams escape them
   statues lose hands faces to a platinum wind
      night coughs snow in the hand of winter
         whispers are wrapped and addressed

4.

then rabbits of snow fall from the hands of statues
   winter unwraps its flowering breath
      infants are blown into cornices with lost dreams
         only avenues without access remain open

1.
when crumbs from light's black bread sink in the water
oaks hide their hands in night's skirts

fingers tie wind into nets to catch sleep
a nail penetrates its reflection

and vessels painted with a thousand eyes
slip into the lily glass

2.
then nuns put white fingers to the wind's lips
their fingers fall on lakes to float among closed lilies

water rises in the grass
wind separates veins from marble

and in all the parks oaks
open their lips and breathe

1.

a fox and a girl meet among stars
   a violin empties itself   the cuckoo calls
      bees hive in the moon enchanted by violins
         in a chapel the rose sheds its shadow

2.

enchanted birches reach for the girl the fox
   the night is a mountain of honey and shadow
      a violin captures the moon in its filaments
         a chapel folds in the girl's hand
            she casts the mountain from her back
                              like a heavy cloak

3.

stars swarm where enchanted roses bloom
   the girl plays her violin for the fox on a road
                              spread with honey
      a birch gathers bees in its shadow
         in the moon's folds the cuckoo sleeps

1.
Garbo's knees are gateposts to violets and chateaux
   directors curl in the veiled moons of mandolins
      it is the one-eyed hour
        it is an evening of ladders

2.
ladders lean on the elephant evening
   closing violets slither across the moon
      a mandolin strikes
        Garbo tosses a star through her veil and runs
                    from the window

3.
stars travel with trunks ladders and apples
   an elephant kissing Garbo is struck by a violet
      when directors float through the absinthe
        gateposts shut

4.
knees with mandolins climb ladders to evening
   violets close on the blade of the hour
      cameras shut their windows
        Garbo curls in the eye of an absinthe moon

1.

evening, wedged in the door like a grand piano, begins to sing
   in its cage a knob
      turns cool with envy
         a bug climbs evening's steps

2.

fastening itself against evening, the door
   hears its hinges sing off key
      canaries lay knobs on steps that climb
         a piano lifts its hat in passing

3.

a canary's key is turned   the key begins singing
   bandages uncurl and chase nasturtiums
      down gutters of brass streets
         the piano trips the canary   the bug passes away

4.

a piano accompanies a nasturtium to her door
   keys curl in keyholes and will not turn
      evening, removing his hat, sings a requiem for a bug
         nasturtiums accompany him on the piano

1.

settling on tongues, owls close their claws
   moles inspect the dark in pulsing passages
      syllables flutter
         then the moon is an owl's eye gliding
               through bone and crystal

2.

behind the moon, fluttering tongues weave legends
   bones glow in the forest of breath
      sorcerers inspect a scent left by the future
         and stars, crystals buried in night's cloak

3.

sorcerers wipe lips with sleeves of fleeing dreams
   behind eyelids the earth revolves, shedding moss
   naked, the earth is a glowing syllable
      in legends bones have lips and breathe

1.

stone tears loosen   they gallop into the canyon
    the bowl of the moon is filled with fish
        when they spill stones open
            and hoofprints flow into emptiness

2.

horses drink the water of the moon
    sometimes they leave footprints in its glowing bowl
        death is a river in night's finger
            emptiness flows through the foot of night

3.

death sinks its empty shaft in a stone
    the moon's coal glows
        in the pipe of dead Indians
            fish climb smoking cliffs to spawn

4.

the moon's feathers loosen and fall
    its naked cheek is printed with hoofs
        a finger puts out the coal
            night closes its canyon

1.

over a forest of coffins morning rings
   telephones open scattering pigeons
      brokers nest in baskets of numbers
         lips splatter the city's wash

2.

prices are picked from morning's ear
   rings open windows and are blown out
      wiping lips, numbers breathe
         telephones appraise the price of a coffin

3.

prices in plush coffins lie
   baskets of brokers leave for tomorrow
      between numbers and coffins the morning washes out
         lips wing for the nearest forest

4.

ears ring with appraisals
   dragging their brokers, telephones scatter
      steel pigeons open
         tomorrow's a forest of holes without coffins

1.

roads slide across towers
   shouts are invisible
      tugged from the sea, lines
         waver and begin to wave
           towers rise peering

2.

gulls circle among the stars
   the blue of the sea is divided
      stars dive from the towers
         and come up voices
           how proudly they wave!

3.

shouts are swallowed by circles
   the road to a tower is picked up
      tooting proudly, tugs tow the horizon
         where flag after flag
           after flag flowers

4.

lines on roads are invisible
   when stars are lined up
      one escapes as a flower
         a flag is a wave
           painted with lines and stars

5.

a gull casts a line for the last star
   and is tugged through

1.

in the half light summits rise
   turtles beat rapids with half packed bags
      snapshots catch their frames on dusty ranges
        watches pack their wrists and beat it
          destiny looks forward to its wake

2.

summits soften
   packing a roomy frame with ranges
      snapshots telescope rooms into one room
        balconies coo from their perch
          years tick on a wrist of dust

3.

turtles climb rapids perching telescopes coo
   years close and catch the next room out
      balconies telescope through half light
        the beat in a wrist transports it
          trains repose in the rapid dust

1.

light pecks the lilacs   they undulate
　　they tumble like stuffed lectures
　　　　crows bury diamonds and gestures in towers
　　　　　　destiny shakes its path at the grass

2.

the mirage saunters down the path in a crow's disguise
　　grass takes the path to the tower
　　　　earth gazes at buried gestures

3.

lilacs shake their ears   mirages fly into them
　　from the tower earth tumbles as an egg
　　　　the egg disguising itself as earth breaks open

4.

destiny takes the guise of a light gesture
　　when the earth shakes lilacs fly into lectures
　　　　diamonds light the path to the earth's egg

5.

towers tumble
　　crows saunter from the broken earth
　　　　earth undulates
　　　　　　the ideal lecture flows in its grassy ears

1.
teeth break against clouds
and their roots fly away

broken pillows rain dɔwn
trousers hitch themselves up laughing

at yawning windows, blouses lean
gossiping with the starlings

2.
geraniums box on the sills
roots untangle aerials and plant them

a boy flies away
pillow stuffed trousers begin laughing

they laugh so hard roaches break out
blouses shrivel   they go *ha ha*

3.
boys stuffed with cereal settle in boxes
let out, trousers blow between windows

blouses yawn
roaches escape on the backs of starlings

geraniums knock their heads together
aerials laugh and laugh

1.

hours knock in the wrists of gypsies
   under flaming skirts beetles scatter like beads
      crossed by deserts, gypsies
         paint an entrance to their palms and fling gold into it
            also nails taken from wounds

2.

at the entrance a cock hangs by its feet
   its tongue drops and grows into a cross of gold
      beetles cross the desert with straws
         between thumb and forefinger flames are extinguished

3.

wrists collect golden beetles
   gypsies hang palms tears tongues at the entrance to their hours
      the cock walks on sons of the nails he hung from
         tears wound the food of wind

4.

under flung straw a desert opens its skirts
   in the cursed zone there are no corners
      beetles are dragged across wounded palms
         and the wind's tongue enters without knocking

1.

leaves sail in the shadow of a pond
   a daisy's petals invade the surrounding whiteness
      the queen in her ship circles a heron

2.

rabbits drop from the clustering afternoon
   in the yellow leaf a pond cradles clouds
      the wind moves through the sky
         drawn by a string in the minnow's mouth
            a shadow swallows a heron

3.

the pond transfixes the sun and its border of white petals
   the queen snips off her shadow
      with the weight of clouds in it the pond can hardly move
         minnows cluster in the queen's whiteness

4.

her extended palm is a ship becalmed in a field
   rabbits scurry across the sky to pin the queen together
      the queen swallows her shadow
         the heron stalks a yellow cloud in the pond
            as though there were no queen   no ship

1.

because a sailor's pockets
  are filled with sea bells
    and the coral whistle
    whistles to itself on the shelf
   where the father's carved bone
oozes a marrow more salt than sweet

   the she of the sea mends her float
and escapes like a duck
   unbuttoning her bouys

2.

    because sea belles call
  sailors into their skirts
and the shelf of the self
breaks on the reefs
   our father' coral bones
     call us to caves   to the marrow

mending the maybe of tomorrow
   against what we see in the sea
buttoned against the deep

bouyant   we duck

1.

locusts older than alphabets
   salt this stable dream   pressed grapes
      merge with the acre's cycle
         and in the membranes of the eldest
         thunder clenches its fist
      as if a storm could replace his sheep
   and return him his teeth
in the cycle of seasons

2.

the zither-girl loiters in the grain
   under thundering skies her song
      rides on the wind polling the sheep
         oh there is a cycle on earth
       an alphabet   five vowels
      and consonant tongues rap on teeth
   as elders stable the flock
that comes to replace them

3.

threshed grain is returned to its acre
   a girl with a zither replaces the eldest
      acres bristle with the alphabet of return
      in the distance locusts hum
   and men sing   trampling grapes
firm as planets

1.

will the poems take off their garments
   and walk naked into the hall of mirrors
      take off their private skins
         and like rivers of nerves hang
            or shrink in the fingers of indifferent men

2.

the poems step from their garments
   and walk naked down endless corridors
      the mirror-streams catch youth
         lost sailing
            the lost do not die

3.

only the certain present is eaten
   or cracks on the pavement
      steps erase steps
         as a cake erases butter and flour
            prints can be lifted and taken

4.

in the museum not one foot with living rivers
   death splits the poem's sail
      only the living wind is left
         youth does not die
            but cracks

5.

and out steps the endless flower   a footstep
   ringing beyond the corridors